Need Money? Ask Me!

Your Guide to Smart Borrowing and Successful
Wealth Creation With Real Estate

Reggie Williams

Copyright © 2024 by Reggie Williams

All rights reserved.

No portion of this book may be reproduced in any form without written permission from the publisher or author, except as permitted by U.S. copyright law.

Contents

Foreword by Joe Stumpf	IV
Overview	VII
1. From Struggle to Strength The Immigrant Mindset	1
2. Navigating the Mortgage Maze Your Path to Homeownership	6
3. The Heart of the Matter Why People Come First	12
4. Cracking the Lending Code Your Guide Through the Mortgage Maze	16
5. The Dream Team Your Homebuying All-Stars	21
6. The Daily Grind How I Make Magic Happen for You	27
7. Faith, Finance, and Finding Your Path The 100-Foot Journey	32

Foreword

by Joe Stumpf

It's with immense pride and a heart full of admiration that I pen this foreword for Reggie Williams' book, "Need Money? Ask Me." As Reggie's business coach for several decades, I've had the privilege of witnessing his remarkable journey from a young man facing adversity to becoming a true pillar of his community and a beacon in the mortgage industry.

Reggie's story is one of resilience, determination, and unwavering faith. I remember clearly the day I first met Reggie. There was a fire in his eyes, a hunger to learn and grow, and a deep-seated desire to make a difference in people's lives. What struck me most was his willingness to embrace challenges head-on, viewing each obstacle as an opportunity for growth.

Over the years, I've watched Reggie transform from a promising professional into a true leader and mentor. His journey hasn't been easy. He's faced setbacks that would have deterred many others, but Reggie's response was always the same: to dig deeper, learn more, and come back stronger.

What sets Reggie apart is not just his formidable professional acumen but also his heart. Reggie genuinely cares about his clients, seeing each mortgage not as a transaction but as a step in someone's life journey. He understands that a home is more than four walls and a roof – it's a foundation for dreams, a safe haven for families, and a cornerstone of financial security.

In this book, Reggie shares the wisdom he's gained through years of experience, personal struggles, and professional triumphs. But more than that, he offers a roadmap for success that goes beyond mortgages and finance. He shows us how to approach life with faith, integrity, and a commitment to continuous growth.

As you read through these chapters, you'll discover:

1. The immigrant mindset that shaped Reggie's work ethic and resilience.

2. How to navigate the thrilling ups and downs of the mortgage process with confidence.

3. The "Reggie Rules" that put people before profit, ensuring client success.

4. Practical wisdom for overcoming financial obstacles and achieving your dreams.

5. The power of building a dream team and the strength found in family connections.

6. How to structure your day for maximum productivity and personal growth.

7. The role of faith and positivity in achieving financial and personal success.

Each chapter is filled with practical advice, inspiring stories, and the kind of hard-earned wisdom that only comes from years of experience and a genuine desire to help others.

I encourage you to not just read this book but to engage with it. Take notes, reflect on the lessons, and, most importantly, take action. If you have the opportunity to work with Reggie, please seize it. You'll not only gain a skilled mortgage professional but also a dedicated advocate for your financial success.

Reggie Williams is more than a successful businessman; he's a mensch – a person of integrity and honor. His journey from struggle to success and his commitment to lifting others as he climbs is an inspiration to us all.

As you turn these pages, you're not just reading a book about mortgages; you're getting to know a remarkable individual who has the knowledge, heart, and faith to guide you toward your dreams of homeownership and financial security.

Reggie, my friend, I couldn't be prouder of the man you've become and the lives you've touched. This book is a testament to your journey, your wisdom, and your unwavering commitment to serving others. May it inspire and guide countless individuals on their own paths to success.

To the readers: Prepare to be inspired, educated, and motivated. Your journey to homeownership and financial empowerment starts here, guided by one of the best in the business. Enjoy the ride!

Joe Stumpf
Founder, By Referral Only

Overview

Chapter 1. From Struggle to Strength: The Immigrant Mindset

You're about to embark on a journey through my life, and I promise it will inspire and guide you through your own financial adventures. In this chapter, you'll discover how my immigrant parents instilled in me a powerful work ethic and resilience that shaped my future. You'll learn how my early challenges, including my parents' divorce and our financial struggles, became the foundation for my deep understanding of the emotional roller coaster you might experience when dealing with mortgages and finances. I'll show you how I transformed adversity into opportunity, developing a unique perspective that allows me to connect with you on a profound level. You'll see how my background gives me the strength to be the mentor and guide that you're looking for in your darkest financial times. By the end of this chapter, you'll understand how my past has equipped me to lead you through your own financial journey, whether you're dealing with low credit scores, high interest, or simply need solid advice about your money.

Chapter 2. Navigating the Mortgage Maze - Your Path to Homeownership

Alright, future homeowner let's dive into the mortgage maze together! Picture the mortgage process as a winding river. It might look chaotic at first, but there's a natural flow to it. Our job? Navigate this river together, avoiding the rapids and finding the smoothest path to your new home.

First things first, we need to understand your current financial situation. It's like checking our supplies before a long journey. We'll map out the major milestones - pre-approval, house hunting, loan application, underwriting, and closing. But here's the kicker - we're not going to rush. A solid pre-approval is your secret weapon in this market.

Now, let's talk about different types of mortgages. Think of these as different boats we could use to navigate our river. Each has its strengths and weaknesses, and we'll find the perfect match for your unique situation.

But it's not just about getting you into a home. We need to look at the big picture - how your mortgage choice impacts your long-term financial health. We'll run different scenarios, play with numbers, and find a solution that sets you up for success.

Remember, things don't always go according to plan. But that's why you've got me as your guide. I've been down this river before, and I know how to handle the unexpected twists and turns.

By the time we're done, you won't just be a homeowner - you'll be a mortgage expert yourself. Ready to start this journey? Let's make some waves!

Chapter 3. The Heart of the Matter: Why People Come First

Hey there, future homeowner! Let's have a heart-to-heart about what really matters in this mortgage business. You see, for me, it's all about putting people before profit. I'm not just here to crunch numbers - I'm here to understand your dreams, your fears, and your unique situation.

Think of me as a tailor for your finances. I don't just whip out a measuring tape - I invite you in, get to know you, and craft a financial solution that fits you perfectly. Sometimes, that means looking beyond the numbers on your credit report and seeing the person behind them.

I remember a client, Jane, who came to me with less-than-perfect credit. Other lenders had shown her the door, but I invited her in. We worked together, improved her credit, and turned her homeownership dream into reality. That's why I do this job - for those moments when you realize you've changed someone's life for the better.

Now, let's talk about the long game. When you work with me, you're not just getting a mortgage broker - you're getting a financial partner for life. Think of me as your personal financial trainer, here to support you long after you've closed on your home.

Remember, buying a home is more than just a financial transaction - it's a life-changing event. And my job is to guide you through that change, to be your support system, your cheerleader, and sometimes, your reality check.

So, are you ready to work with someone who sees you as more than just a number on an application? Let's turn your homeownership dreams into reality the right way!

Chapter 4. Cracking the Lending Code: Your Guide Through the Mortgage Maze

Now, it's time to pull back the curtain and show you how the mortgage magic really happens. Think of this as your backstage pass to the lending world. We're not just talking numbers here - we're talking about turning your dreams into reality.

Remember, understanding your income isn't just about glancing at a pay stub. It's about diving deep, asking the right questions, and sometimes, reading between the lines. I once had a client, a schoolteacher, whose summer school earnings were the key to unlocking her dream home. That's the kind of detail we don't miss.

Now, let's talk about documentation. I know it's not the most exciting topic. But trust me, in the right hands, those piles of paperwork can be your secret weapon. It's not just about ticking boxes - it's about telling your financial story in a way that makes lenders sit up and take notice.

Obstacles? Yeah, we'll face them. But I've never met an obstacle I couldn't overcome. Whether it's a tricky credit situation or an unusual income source, we'll find a way. Remember, these aren't dead ends - they're just opportunities to get creative.

And here's something you might not expect - we're going to celebrate along the way. Every milestone, no matter how small, is worth recognizing. Because this journey isn't just about buying a house - it's about building your confidence, your financial savvy, and your future.

So, are you ready to crack the lending code? Let's turn the complex world of mortgages into your personal path to homeownership!

Chapter 5. Building Your Dream Team: The Power of Family and Connections

In this chapter, you'll get an insider's look at the exceptional team I've assembled to support your journey to homeownership. You'll meet each member of my carefully curated group, from my daughter Sierra to my processing team, and understand the unique strengths they bring to the table. Discover how my family-oriented approach extends beyond my immediate family to create a cohesive, committed team that works tirelessly on your behalf. You'll learn about the values that bind our team together, such as connection, commitment, flexibility, and putting clients first. By the end of this chapter, you'll understand why having my team in your corner is like having an entire family rooting for your success. You'll see how our combined expertise, dedication, and shared values create a synergy that benefits you at every stage of the mortgage process. You'll also gain insights into how you can apply similar principles to build your own dream team in various aspects of your life.

Chapter 6. The Daily Grind: How I Make Magic Happen for You

Step into my world and discover the daily rituals and routines that fuel my success and, ultimately, benefit you as my client. In this chapter, you'll learn about my unique approach to structuring my day, with proactive mornings focused on personal growth and preparation, followed by reactive afternoons dedicated to client service. You'll see how practices like meditation, physical exercise, and journaling contribute to the clarity and energy I bring to every interaction with you. Discover the power of my to-do lists and how my disciplined approach ensures that nothing falls through the cracks in your mortgage process. By the end of this chapter, you'll understand how my personal habits translate into professional excellence, and you'll be inspired to implement some of these practices in your own life. You'll appreciate how my commitment to self-improvement and balance allows me to show up as the best version of myself for you every day.

Chapter 7. Faith, Finance, and Finding Your Path: The 100-Foot Journey

In this final chapter, you'll explore the spiritual foundation that underlies my approach to business and life. I'll share how my faith forms my perspective on money. You'll learn about what I call the "headlight metaphor" and how it applies to your financial journey – focusing on the next 100 feet while trusting in the ultimate destination. I'll explain my belief in the power of choice, particularly choosing happiness and love in the face of challenges. You'll see how this mindset translates into my positive, solution-oriented approach to even the most complex financial situations. By the end of this chapter, you'll understand how my faith and philosophy can inspire your own approach to money and life. You'll be equipped with a new perspective on your financial journey, seeing it as part of a larger path of personal growth and purpose. Whether you share my specific beliefs or not, you'll appreciate the value of having a guide whose actions are rooted in deep-seated principles and a genuine desire to help you succeed.

Chapter One

From Struggle to Strength

The Immigrant Mindset

The Roots of Resilience

Picture this: a crisp Miami morning, the sun just peeking over the horizon, painting the sky in hues of orange and pink. That's where our story begins, not with me but with two courageous souls who left everything behind in Jamaica to chase the American dream. Those two? They're my parents, and their story is the foundation of mine.

Now, you might be wondering, "Reggie, what's this got to do with mortgages?" Well, stick with me, because the journey we're about to begin will change the way you think about money, success, and what's possible in your life.

You see, my parents didn't just bring suitcases when they came to America. They brought something far more valuable - the immigrant mindset. It's a potent mix of grit, determination, and a work ethic that just won't quit. And let me tell you, that mindset; It's been the secret ingredient in every success I've had.

Growing up, I watched my dad, an electronic engineer at BellSouth, push himself to the limit every single day. But here's the kicker - his day job wasn't enough. He always had a side hustle going, whether it was fixing things around the neighborhood or picking up extra gigs. And my mom? She jumped into the workforce, too, both of them laser-focused on giving us a shot at a better life.

The Power of Observation

Now, I want you to imagine yourself in my shoes for a moment. Picture yourself as a kid, watching your parents hustle day in and day out. What do you think that teaches you? For me, it hammered home one crucial lesson: success isn't something that falls into your lap. You've got to work for it, and when obstacles pop up, you don't throw in the towel. You find a way around them, over them, or straight through them.

But life, as you know, has a funny way of throwing curveballs when you least expect them. For me, that curveball came whistling in when I was about ten years old. My parents divorced, and just like that, the stable family life I knew vanished like smoke in the wind.

I'm not going to sugarcoat it - this was a tough time. One day, I had a father figure in the house, and the next? Gone. Like many kids in that situation, I found myself looking for direction from neighbors, friends, and people who, if I'm honest, were often just as lost as I was.

But here's where it gets interesting. That experience, as painful as it was, taught me something crucial: life is unpredictable, and you need to be adaptable. It's a lesson that's served me well in the mortgage industry, and it's one that I'm going to use to help you navigate the ups and downs of your own financial journey.

The Financial Wake-Up Call

Now, remember how I said life throws curveballs? Well, it wasn't done with me yet. As if the emotional rollercoaster wasn't enough, our family got hit with a financial crisis that would make anyone's head spin. My mom, bless her heart, has always struggled with managing money. Even today, her relationship with finances is... let's just say it's complicated.

This struggle led to our house going into foreclosure when I was a teenager. Can you imagine that? The stress of potentially losing your home at that age? It was like a bucket of ice-cold reality dumped right over my head.

But here's where the story takes an interesting turn. A man named Dustin Gold stepped into our lives. He was in the mortgage industry and managed to refinance our house, saving it from foreclosure. He eventually became my mother's boyfriend and was like a stepfather.

Now, you might be thinking, "Okay, Reggie, that's quite a story, but what's it got to do with me?" Well, let me tell you - this experience was the spark that ignited my passion for mortgages. Watching Dustin work his magic with our family's finances? It was like seeing a magician pull a rabbit out of a hat. It opened my eyes to the power of understanding money and mortgages. It showed me how knowledge in this field can literally save homes and change lives.

The Golden Rules of Finance

From the age of 16, I started picking Dustin's brain about finances, relationships, and the power of asking the right questions. He taught me what I now call the "Golden Rules" of finance - principles that guide my work to this day and that I'm going to share with you.

One of the most important lessons I learned was the power of inquiry. Dustin showed me that asking the right questions can reveal information people don't usually volunteer. This skill? It's invaluable in my work today, helping me to understand your unique financial situation and find the best solutions for you.

Another crucial lesson was about the relationship people have with money. Seeing my mom's struggles and contrasting them with Dustin's expertise showed me how a healthy understanding of finances can make all the difference in a person's life. That's why I'm not just here to get you a mortgage - I'm here to help you develop a better relationship with your money.

Now, you might be thinking, "Reggie, that's a lot of hardship. How did you turn all of that into something positive?" And that's a great question.

Turning Adversity into Advantage

You see, all these experiences - the immigrant work ethic from my parents, the adaptability I learned from my parent's divorce, and the financial literacy I gained from our near-foreclosure experience - all came together to shape who I am today.

I've taken all this wisdom and awareness and brought it into the mortgage business. When you work with me, you're not just getting a mortgage broker. You're getting someone who understands the emotional roller coaster of financial stress. Someone who knows what it's like to face the possibility of losing a home. Someone who has learned, through personal experience, how to turn financial challenges into opportunities.

At this point, you might be wondering, "That's an interesting story, Reggie, but how does this help me?"

Well, let me break it down for you. It helps you in more ways than you might realize.

First, it means I truly understand where you're coming from. Whether you're dealing with a low credit score, struggling with high interest rates, or just need some solid advice about your money, I've been there. I've seen it. And more importantly, I've learned how to overcome it.

Why This Matters for You

Secondly, it means I can provide you with real, practical guidance. The lessons I've learned aren't just theory - they're tried and tested in the real world. When I give you advice, it's coming from a place of genuine experience and understanding.

Lastly, and perhaps most importantly, it means I'm committed to your success. I know firsthand how much of a difference the right financial guidance can make in a person's life. That's why I'm not just here to process your mortgage application. I'm here to be your mentor, your guide, and your advocate throughout your financial journey.

As we wrap up this chapter, I want you to remember one thing: no matter where you are in your financial journey right now, there's always a path forward. Whether you're looking to buy your first home, refinance your current mortgage, or just get a better handle on your finances, I'm here to help you find that path.

In the chapters that follow, we're going to dive deep into the world of mortgages and finance. We'll explore strategies for navigating the lending process, tips for improving your financial health, and insights into how you can make your money work harder for you.

The Road Ahead

But more than that, we're going to work on changing your relationship with money. Just like I learned to do all those years ago, you're going to discover how to approach your finances with confidence, knowledge, and a positive mindset.

Remember, your financial story is still being written. And just like I did, you have the power to turn any financial challenges into stepping stones toward a brighter future. Are you ready to take that journey with me? Let's get started!

Chapter Two

Navigating the Mortgage Maze

Your Path to Homeownership

As the first rays of sunlight crept through your window, you couldn't help but feel a mix of excitement and apprehension. Today was the day you'd finally take the plunge into the world of mortgages and homeownership. You'd heard stories - some triumphant, others cautionary - but now it was your turn to write your own tale.

Little did you know, I, Reggie Williams, was already up and preparing for our meeting. I'd spent years honing my skills in the mortgage industry, learning its ins and outs, its peaks and valleys. But more importantly, I'd learned how to guide people like you through this complex landscape.

As you stepped into my office, I could see the determination in your eyes, mixed with a hint of uncertainty. "Welcome," I said, gesturing to a comfortable chair. "I know this process can seem overwhelming, but I promise you, by the time we're done, you'll feel like a mortgage expert yourself."

You settled into the chair, notebook in hand, ready to embark on this journey. I couldn't help but smile, remembering my own first steps into this world.

"Let's start at the beginning," I said, leaning forward. "Imagine the mortgage process as a winding river. It may seem chaotic at first glance, but there's a natural flow to it. Our job is to navigate this river together, avoiding the rapids and finding the smoothest path to your new home."

I could see you relax a bit at this analogy. Good. A calm mind is crucial for making the best decisions.

"The first bend in our river," I continued, "is understanding your current financial situation. It's like checking our supplies before a long journey. We need to know exactly what we're working with."

For the next hour, we dove deep into your finances. We talked about your income, your debts, your savings. With each revelation, I could see the fog of uncertainty lifting from your eyes. Knowledge is power, and you were becoming more powerful by the minute.

"Now," I said, pulling out a large sheet of paper, "let's map out our journey." I began sketching out the major milestones of the mortgage process - pre-approval, house hunting, loan application, underwriting, and closing.

"See this part here?" I pointed to the space between pre-approval and house hunting. "This is where many people rush. They get excited and jump into looking at houses before they're truly ready. But we're going to do things differently."

I explained how a solid pre-approval could set you apart from other buyers. "In this market," I said, "a strong pre-approval is like having a secret weapon. It shows sellers you're serious and capable of following through."

As we discussed the pre-approval process, I could see a question forming in your mind. "But Reggie," you asked, "what if my credit isn't perfect? I've heard horror stories about people being denied mortgages over a few late payments."

I smiled, appreciating your candor. "That's a great question," I replied. "And it's true, credit is important. But it's not the only factor. Let me tell you a story about a client I had a few years back."

I recounted the tale of Jane, a young professional whose credit had taken a hit due to some medical bills. She thought homeownership was out of reach, but we worked together to find a solution. We focused on her strong income, her steady job history, and her substantial savings. In the end, we secured her a great mortgage rate.

"The point is," I concluded, "there's almost always a path forward. It might not be the path we initially expected, but that's why I'm here - to help you find the way."

You nodded with a new spark of hope in your eyes.

Next, we explored the different types of mortgages. "Think of these as different boats we could use to navigate our river," I explained. "Each has its strengths and weaknesses."

We discussed fixed-rate mortgages, adjustable-rate mortgages, FHA loans, VA loans, and more. With each option, I provided real-world examples of how they had worked for past clients.

"Remember," I said, "there's no one-size-fits-all solution in mortgages. What works for your neighbor might not be the best fit for you. Our job is to find the perfect match for your unique situation."

As we explored these options, I could see the wheels turning in your head. You were starting to see mortgages not as a necessary evil but as a tool - a means to achieve your dreams.

"Now," I said, leaning back in my chair, "let's talk about something that many people overlook - the long-term impact of your mortgage choice."

I pulled out a calculator and began running some numbers. "Let's say we're looking at a $300,000 home. With a 30-year fixed-rate mortgage at 6.5%, your monthly payment would be about $1,347, not including taxes and insurance."

You nodded, following along.

"But what if we could get you a 15-year mortgage at 6%? Your monthly payment would increase to about $2,071, but..." I paused for effect, "You'd save over $120,000 in interest over the life of the loan."

Your eyes widened at this revelation. "That's... a lot of money," you said softly.

"Exactly," I replied. "And that's why it's so important to look at the big picture. Sometimes, what seems more expensive in the short term can save you a fortune in the long run."

We spent the next hour exploring different scenarios, playing with numbers, and discussing how each choice could impact your financial future. With each calculation, I could see you becoming more engaged and more excited about the possibilities.

"But Reggie," you interjected at one point, "all of this assumes the process goes smoothly. What if something goes wrong? What if the appraisal comes in low, or the inspection reveals problems?"

I nodded appreciatively. "Those are excellent questions. And you're right - things don't always go according to plan. But that's why it's so important to have a guide who's been down this river before."

I shared stories of past clients who had faced challenges - a low appraisal that threatened to derail a deal, a last-minute job change that spooked the underwriters, and unexpected repairs that popped up during inspection. With each tale, I explained how we navigated these obstacles, finding creative solutions and keeping the process on track.

"The key," I said, "is to anticipate potential issues and have a plan in place. It's like packing a life jacket for our river journey. We hope we won't need it, but we'll be glad to have it if we do."

As our meeting stretched into its third hour, I could see that you were starting to feel more confident and more in control. The mortgage process was no longer a daunting mystery but a challenge you were ready to tackle.

"Before we wrap up," I said, "I want to talk about something that often gets overlooked in the excitement of buying a home - your life after the purchase."

You leaned forward, intrigued.

"Buying a home is a huge achievement," I continued, "but it's also the beginning of a new financial chapter in your life. We need to make sure you're set up for long-term success."

We discussed budgeting for home maintenance, the importance of building an emergency fund, and strategies for continuing to grow your wealth even as you pay down your mortgage.

"Remember," I said, "a house is more than just a place to live. It's an investment in your future. And with the right approach, it can be a powerful tool for building long-term wealth."

As our meeting came to a close, I could see a transformation had taken place. The uncertainty in your eyes had been replaced with determination. The apprehension in your posture had given way to excitement.

"So," I said, standing up and extending my hand, "are you ready to start this journey?"

You stood as well, grasping my hand firmly. "Absolutely," you replied, a confident smile spreading across your face.

As you turned to leave, I called out one last time. "Remember," I said, "this isn't a journey you have to make alone. I'll be right here with you every step of the way."

You nodded, gratitude evident in your eyes, and stepped out into the world - not just as a potential homebuyer but as an informed, empowered individual ready to navigate the mortgage maze and achieve your dreams of homeownership.

As I watched you go, I couldn't help but feel a sense of pride and excitement. Another journey was beginning, and another story of homeownership was about to be written. And I, Reggie Williams, was honored to play a part in it.

In the world of mortgages and homeownership, every day brings new challenges and opportunities. But with the right knowledge, the right guidance, and the right attitude, there's no obstacle that can't be overcome, no dream that can't be achieved.

So, here's to you, future homeowner. Here's to the journey ahead, to the challenges we'll face, and the victories we'll celebrate. Here's to turning the dream of homeownership into a reality, one step at a time.

Welcome to your mortgage journey. The adventure is just beginning.

Chapter Three

The Heart of the Matter

Why People Come First

Hey there, future homeowner! You've made it this far, and I couldn't be prouder. Now, let's sit down and have a heart-to-heart about what really matters in this whole mortgage business. I'm Reggie Williams, and I'm about to share with you the core of my philosophy - why I always put people before profit.

Imagine you're walking into a tailor's shop. The moment you step through the door, the tailor doesn't just whip out a measuring tape. Instead, he invites you to sit down, offers you a cup of coffee, and starts asking about your life. Where do you work? What's your style? What's the occasion for this new suit?

That's exactly how I approach mortgages. You see, I believe that understanding you - your dreams, your fears, your unique situation - is the key to finding the perfect financial fit. It's not just about numbers on a page; it's about the story behind those numbers.

I remember a client, let's call her Jane. She came to me, eyes downcast, mumbling about her less-than-perfect credit score. Other lenders had shown her the door, but I invited her in. We sat down, and I asked her to tell me her story.

Turns out, Jane had been laid off a few years back. She'd struggled to make ends meet, and her credit had taken a hit. But now she was back on her feet, with a stable job and a dream of owning a home. As she spoke, I didn't just hear words - I felt her determination, her hope, and, yes, her fear of being rejected again.

That's when I knew we had to make this work. Not because it was a big commission - trust me, there are easier ways to make money in this business. No, we had to make it work because Jane deserved a chance. She deserved someone who would look beyond the numbers and see the person behind them.

We spent the next few months working together. I helped her understand her credit report, gave her tips to improve her score, and kept her motivated when things got tough. It wasn't always easy, but Jane was committed, and so was I.

Fast forward a year, and there was Jane, keys in hand, standing on the porch of her very own home. The smile on her face? That's why I do this job. It's not about the paycheck; it's about the lives we change.

Now, let me tell you about another client, John. John came to me all confident, waving around a pre-approval letter from another lender. He was ready to go house hunting right away. But something didn't sit right with me. The numbers seemed off.

I could have just gone along with it. After all, John was eager to buy, and that meant a quick commission for me. But that's not how I operate. Instead, I sat John down and asked him to walk me through his finances.

Turns out that pre-approval was based on some overly optimistic assumptions. If John had gone through with it, he would have been house-poor, struggling to make payments each month. It would have turned his dream home into a nightmare.

So, we pumped the brakes. We looked at his budget, his long-term goals, and his lifestyle. We ran different scenarios and considered various loan options. In the end, we found a solution that allowed John to buy a home he loved without sacrificing his financial stability.

Was it more work for me? Absolutely. Did it delay the process? You bet. But it was the right thing to do. Because at the end of the day, I'm not here to sell you a mortgage. I'm here to help you build a better life.

This brings me to something I call the "long game." You see, many folks in this industry are focused on the quick win - get you into a mortgage, collect the commission, and move on to the next client. But that's not my style.

When you work with me, you're not just getting a mortgage broker. You're getting a financial partner for life. Think of me as your personal financial trainer. Just like a good trainer doesn't abandon you after you've lost those first 10 pounds, I don't disappear after you've closed on your home.

Now, let's talk about something that might seem a bit odd in the financial world - emotions. Yep, you heard me right. Emotions play a huge role in the homebuying process and ignoring them is like trying to bake a cake without flour.

I remember working with a couple, Tom and Lisa. They were first-time homebuyers, excited but also terrified. Every step of the process brought a new worry. What if we can't afford it? What if we lose our jobs? What if the roof caves in the day after we move in?

Some brokers might have brushed off these concerns or, worse, taken advantage of them to push a more expensive product. But not me. Instead, we tackled each fear head-on. We created a budget that included a hefty emergency fund. We looked at job loss insurance. We even brought in a home inspector to give them a crash course in home maintenance.

By the time we got to closing day, Tom and Lisa weren't just financially prepared - they were emotionally ready for homeownership. And let me tell you, the peace of mind on their faces was worth more than any commission.

Here's the thing - buying a home is more than a financial transaction. It's a life-changing event. And my job isn't just to crunch numbers; it's to guide you through that change, to be your support system, your cheerleader, and sometimes, your reality check.

So, when you work with me, expect questions, Lots of them. Expect me to dig deep, to challenge your assumptions, to push you to think beyond just the next few years. Expect honesty, even when it's not what you want to hear. And expect dedication - to your goals, your dreams, and your long-term success.

Because, at the end of the day, this isn't about mortgages. It's about people. It's about you. Your hopes, your fears, your future. And there's nothing I take more seriously than that.

So, are you ready to embark on this journey? Are you prepared to work with someone who sees you as more than just a number on an application? If so, then let's get started. Together, we'll navigate the complex world of mortgages, overcome any obstacles in our path, and turn your homeownership dreams into reality.

Remember, in this journey, you're not just a client - you're a partner. And I'm here to support you every step of the way, today, tomorrow, and for years to come. Let's make your homeownership dreams come true the right way!

Chapter Four

Cracking the Lending Code

Your Guide Through the Mortgage Maze

Hey there, future homeowner! You've made it to the heart of our journey together. I'm Reggie Williams and today, we're going to unravel the mysteries of the lending world. Think of this as your backstage pass to the mortgage show - I'm going to pull back the curtain and show you how the magic really happens.

Let me start with a story that'll give you a taste of what we're dealing with. A few years back, I had a client named Sofia. She was a school teacher, smart as a whip, but when it came to mortgages, she felt like she was trying to read hieroglyphics. Sofia came to me with a pre-approval from another lender, but something didn't sit right.

As we sat down in my office, surrounded by stacks of mortgage guidelines (my bedtime reading, if you can believe it), I started asking Sofia about her income. Turns out, the other lender had overlooked her summer school earnings - a sizeable chunk of change that could significantly boost her buying power.

This, my friend, is where the real work begins. You see, understanding income isn't just about glancing at a pay stub. It's about diving deep, asking the right questions, and sometimes, reading between the lines. In Sofia's case, those summer school paychecks were the key to unlocking her dream home.

We spent the next hour poring over her pay stubs, tax returns, and employment contract. By the time we were done, we had painted a complete picture of Sofia's earning power - one that showed she could afford more house than she ever thought possible.

The look on Sofia's face when I told her she could qualify for her dream home? That's why I do this job. It's not about the paycheck; it's about those moments when you realize you've changed someone's life for the better.

Now, let's talk about something that sends shivers down the spines of many homebuyers: documentation. I know it's not the most exciting topic. But trust me, in the right hands, those piles of paperwork can be your secret weapon.

I had a client once, let's call him Mike. Mike was a freelancer, and his income was about as predictable as the weather in April. When he first came to me, he was convinced no lender would touch him with a ten-foot pole. But I saw an opportunity where others saw a problem.

We sat down at my desk, and I pulled out a large whiteboard. "Alright, Mike," I said, "let's map out your financial life." For the next two hours, we created a visual masterpiece. We charted his income streams, tracked his business expenses, and highlighted his savings habits. By the time we were done, that whiteboard told a compelling story of financial responsibility and entrepreneurial success.

When we submitted Mike's application, we included a photo of that whiteboard along with a detailed letter explaining his financial situation. The underwriter later told me it was one of the most comprehensive and clear applications they'd ever seen. John got approved, and he's now running his business from the home office of his dreams.

The lesson here? Documentation isn't just about ticking boxes. It's about telling your financial story in a way that makes lenders sit up and take notice. In the right hands, those papers become a powerful narrative of your creditworthiness.

Now, let's talk about something that keeps many would-be homeowners up at night: obstacles. In my years in this business, I've seen it all. Credit scores that look like they've taken a nosedive off a cliff. Debt-to-income ratios that make accountants wince. Unusual sources of income that make underwriters scratch their heads. But here's the thing - I've never met an obstacle I couldn't overcome.

Take Lisa, for example. Lisa came to me with a credit score that had seen better days, thanks to some medical bills that had gone to collections. Most lenders would have shown her the door, but I saw a fighter who'd been through a tough time and was ready for a fresh start.

We rolled up our sleeves and got to work. First, we disputed some errors on her credit report - you'd be amazed at how common those are. Then, we crafted a heartfelt letter explaining the circumstances behind those medical bills. But we didn't stop there. We also put together a budget showing how Lisa had turned her financial life around since recovering from her illness.

It wasn't an easy road. We faced rejections, and we had to answer what felt like a million questions from underwriters. But we persevered. And six months later, Lisa was moving into her new home, tears of joy streaming down her face as she turned the key for the first time.

That's the thing about obstacles in the mortgage world - they're not dead ends. They're just opportunities to get creative, to show your determination, and to prove that you're more than just a number on a credit report.

Let's switch gears and talk about something that might seem a bit odd in the world of finance: celebration. That's right, I said celebration. You see,

I believe the journey to homeownership should be filled with just as much joy as the destination.

I remember working with a young couple, Tom and Emily. They were first-time homebuyers, and they were nervous as can be. Every step of the process felt like a mountain to them. So, I decided to change the game.

We created a homebuying vision board together, complete with pictures of their dream home features and quotes about the joys of homeownership. Each time we completed a stage of the process - pre-approval, house hunting, offer acceptance - we added a big gold star to the board.

You should have seen their faces light up each time they earned a new star. By the time we got to closing day, that board was shining brighter than Times Square on New Year's Eve. And you know what? Those little celebrations made the whole process feel less like a chore and more like an exciting journey.

That's why I always tell my clients: don't wait until closing day to pop the champagne. Celebrate every milestone, no matter how small. Got your pre-approval? That's worth a fancy dinner out. Found a house you love? Time for a happy dance. Offer accepted? Call your friends and share the news! These moments of joy aren't just fun - they keep you motivated and remind you why you started this journey in the first place.

Now, let's talk about something that's close to my heart: the long game. You see, some folks in this industry are all about the quick win. Get you into a mortgage, collect the commission, sayonara. But that's not how I operate. When you work with me, you're not just getting a mortgage broker - you're getting a lifelong financial partner.

I had a client, Jennifer, who called me five years after buying her first home. She'd just gotten a big promotion and was thinking about upgrading to a larger house. Now, I could have jumped at the chance to broker another mortgage. But instead, we sat down and looked at the big picture.

We crunched the numbers, considered her long-term career goals, and you know what we realized? Refinancing her current home and doing some renovations was actually a better move for her long-term financial health. Did that mean less commission for me compared to a new home purchase? Sure. But it was the right move for Jennifer, and that's what mattered.

Because here's the thing - my goal isn't just to get you into a home. It's to help you build a stable, prosperous financial future. Sometimes that means buying a house. Sometimes, it means waiting. Sometimes, it means looking at options you hadn't even considered. But always, always, it means putting your best interests first.

As we wrap up this chapter, I want to leave you with one final thought. The world of mortgages and lending can seem complex, intimidating, and even a bit scary at times. But with the right guide by your side, it can also be an exciting journey of discovery - about the housing market, yes, but also about yourself.

Through this process, you'll learn about your financial strengths and weaknesses. You'll clarify your goals and priorities. You'll discover reserves of patience and perseverance you never knew you had. And at the end of it all, you'll not only have a new home - you'll have a new level of financial savvy that will serve you for the rest of your life.

So, are you ready to crack the lending code? Are you prepared to navigate the mortgage maze with confidence and clarity? If so, then let's get started. Together, we'll turn the complex world of mortgages into your personal path to homeownership.

Remember, in this journey, you're not just a client - you're a partner. And I'm here to support you every step of the way, today, tomorrow, and for years to come. Let's make your homeownership dreams come true the smart way!

Chapter Five

The Dream Team

Your Homebuying All-Stars

You've made it this far, and I couldn't be prouder. Now, it's time for you to meet the MVPs who'll be backing you up on this incredible journey. I'm Reggie Williams and today, I'm going to introduce you to my dream team – a group of professionals, including my own family members, who are as committed to your success as I am.

You know, when I first started in this business, I thought I could do it all on my own. Man, was I wrong! It didn't take long for me to realize that to truly serve my clients, I needed a team of experts, each bringing their unique skills to the table. So, I set out to build not just any team but a dream team.

Let's talk about Sofia, a first-time homebuyer who recently worked with us. Sofia came to me feeling overwhelmed and a bit scared. She'd been saving for years for a down payment, but the thought of navigating the homebuying process kept her up at night. Little did she know, she was about to meet a group of people who would change her life.

First up, there's my daughter, Sierra. Now, don't let her youth fool you – Sierra's got a gift for making people feel at ease. When Sofia walked into our office, looking like she might bolt at any second, it was Sierra who greeted her with a warm smile and a cup of coffee. "Don't worry," Sierra said, "we've got your back."

Throughout Sofia's journey, Sierra was her go-to person for any questions or concerns. Need an update on your application? Sierra's on it. Feeling anxious about the process? Sierra's there with a pep talk and a funny meme to lighten the mood. By the time we got to closing day, Sofia told me she felt like she'd gained not just a home but a friend.

Next, let me introduce you to my son, Jordan. At 23, Jordan's one of the youngest real estate brokers in Palm Beach, but don't let his age fool you. This kid's got hustle and heart in spades. When Sofia mentioned she was having trouble finding homes in her price range, Jordan jumped into action.

He didn't just send Sofia listings – he went on a mission. Jordan drove around neighborhoods, talked to locals, and used every tech tool at his disposal to find hidden gems. One day, he called Sofia excited: "I think I've found your dream home!" he said. Turns out, he was right. The house Jordan found is where Sofia lives today.

Now, let's talk about my wife, Michelle. While she focuses more on commercial real estate, her expertise is like a secret weapon for our residential clients. When the appraisal on Sofia's dream home came in lower than expected, it was Michelle who saved the day.

She pored over the appraisal report, comparing it with recent sales in the area. "This doesn't add up," she said, brow frowned in concentration. Michelle put together a compelling case for a higher valuation, using her years of experience to highlight factors the appraiser had overlooked. Thanks to her efforts, we got a revised appraisal that made the deal work.

Behind the scenes, we've got our dynamic processing duo, Michelle and Mark. These siblings are like the engine room of a luxury yacht – you might not see them, but boy, do you feel their impact!investor

When Sofia's application hit a snag due to some inconsistencies in her income documentation (it turns out being a teacher with summer school gigs can complicate things), Michelle and Mark were on the case. They didn't just process the paperwork – they became detectives, piecing together Sofia's financial story in a way that made sense to the underwriters.

Every day, Michelle and Mark have a 45-minute debrief session where they review every single file. It's like a daily strategy meeting focused entirely on getting our clients to the finish line. When they tackled Sofia's file, they didn't just solve the income documentation issue – they anticipated and addressed a dozen other potential questions an underwriter might have. By the time Sofia's file reached underwriting, it was bulletproof.

Now, let me tell you about Steve Richards. Steve's story is special because he used to sit where you're sitting now – as a client. A few years back, Steve came to me looking to buy his first home. Fast forward to today, and he's not just a homeowner; he's a key player on our team.

Steve's experience as a former client gives him a unique perspective. When Sofia expressed anxiety about the process, Steve was able to say, "I get it. I've been there." He shared his own homebuying story with Sofia, the ups and downs, and how it all worked out in the end. It was like having a homebuying buddy who'd already walked the path.

Last but definitely not least, we've got our legal eagles. Now, I won't name them individually, but let me tell you, these folks are the unsung heroes of many a homebuying journey. They're like the airbags in your car – you hope you never need them, but you're damn glad they're there if you do.

In Sofia's case, our legal team swooped in when a question arose about the property's title history. There was a potential lien from decades ago that hadn't been properly cleared. Now, this is the kind of thing that can derail a deal if not handled properly. But our legal team? They were on it like white on rice.

They dug through old county records, made calls to track down the original lien holder (who, as it turns out, had long forgotten about this), and ultimately got the issue resolved. Sofia never even knew there was a problem until it was already solved. That's the kind of peace of mind our legal team provides.

Now, you might be wondering, "Reggie, why are you telling me about your family members on the team?" Well, let me share a little secret with you. When your work is also a family business, you bring a different level of commitment to the table. It's not just about closing deals – it's about building a legacy of trust and excellence.

Take our family dinners, for example. Most families might talk about their day or the latest TV show. At our house? We're brainstorming ways to serve our clients better. I remember one Sunday dinner where we were all discussing Sofia's case. Jordan had just found the perfect house for her, and we were all excited.

My wife Michelle said, "You know, with interest rates the way they are, we might be able to get Sofia an even better deal." That sparked a whole conversation about different loan products and strategies. By the end of dinner, we had a new game plan that ended up saving Sofia thousands over the life of her loan.

That's the power of having a family team. We don't clock out at the end of the day. Your success is our success, and we're invested in it 24/7.

But here's the thing – while we're a family business, our definition of family extends to you, our client. When you work with us, you're not just getting a team of professionals. You're becoming part of our extended family. We'll care for your financial future as if it were our own.

Now, let me tell you how all of this came together for Sofia. Remember how nervous she was at the beginning? Well, by the time we got to closing day, Sofia was a different person. She walked into that closing room with her head held high, confident and excited.

As we sat around the closing table, I looked around and saw my dream team in action. Sierra was there, giving Sofia a reassuring smile. Jordan was explaining some last-minute details about the property. My wife Michelle was reviewing the final numbers, making sure everything was perfect. Michelle and Mark from our processing team had put together a closing package so thoroughly that the closing agent commented on how smoothly everything was going.

Steve was there too, remembering his own closing day and sharing in Sofia's excitement. And while our legal team wasn't physically present, their work behind the scenes ensured that this day went off without a hitch.

As Sofia signed that final document and Jordan handed her the keys to her new home, I felt a swell of pride – not just in Sofia's accomplishment but in my team. This is why we do what we do. This is why we've built this family business. To see the joy on Sofia's face, to know that we've helped her achieve a dream – there's no feeling like it in the world.

But our relationship with Sofia didn't end at the closing table. A few weeks later, Sierra called to check in on how Sofia was settling into her new home. A month after that, Jordan helped Sofia find a great contractor for some minor renovations she wanted to do. And when tax season rolled around, Steve was there to help Sofia understand the tax implications of her new homeowner status.

You see, when you work with us, you're not just getting help with one transaction. You're gaining a lifelong financial support system. Imagine five years from now, when you're considering a refinance or looking to purchase an investment property. You'll have a whole team of experts who know your financial history, understand your goals, and are ready to spring into action on your behalf.

Or picture yourself at a family gathering, confidently explaining the home-buying process to a younger relative because of the knowledge you've gained from our multigenerational team. You're not just a homeowner now – you're a financially savvy individual with a powerful network at your fingertips.

That's the power of working with a dream team like ours. We're not just here to get you a mortgage – we're here to empower you, educate you, and support you in your journey to long-term financial success.

So, are you ready to join our extended family? Are you excited to experience the power of a true dream team in your homebuying journey? If so, then let's get started. Together, we'll not just secure your dream home – we'll set you on a path to financial success that can benefit you and your loved ones for years to come.

Remember, in the world of mortgages and homeownership, you're never alone. With our dream team by your side, you've got a whole family of experts ready to turn your homeownership dreams into reality. Let's make some magic happen – for this generation and the next!

Chapter Six

The Daily Grind

How I Make Magic Happen for You

Hey there, future homeowner! You've met my dream team, and now it's time to pull back the curtain and show you how the magic really happens. I'm Reggie Williams, and today, I'm going to walk you through a day in my life. But this isn't just about me – it's about how every minute of my day is laser-focused on turning your homeownership dreams into reality.

Let me tell you about a client I had recently – we'll call her Isabella. Isabella was a single mom, working two jobs and dreaming of giving her kids a backyard to play in. When she first came to me, she was exhausted, overwhelmed, and not sure if homeownership was even possible for her. But by the end of our journey together, not only did Isabella get her home, but she also gained a whole new level of financial confidence.

So, how did we make that happen? It all starts with my daily routine.

My day kicks off at 5:00 AM sharp. Now, I know what you're thinking – "Reggie, are you crazy? Why on earth would you wake up that early?" Well, let me tell you, these early morning hours are like pure gold. While the rest of the world is still sleeping, I'm up, sharpening my tools and getting ready to champion your cause.

At 5:15 AM, you'll find me on my meditation cushion. Now, I know meditation might sound a bit woo-woo, especially when we're talking about mortgages. But trust me, this quiet time is crucial. It's like clearing out all the junk files in my mental computer, making sure I'm running at peak performance for you.

I remember one morning, as I was sitting there in the quiet, a solution to Isabella's complex income situation suddenly popped into my head. You see, as a gig worker, her income was all over the place, making it tough to qualify for a traditional mortgage. But in that moment of clarity, I realized we could use a bank statement loan program that would work perfectly for her situation. That 40-minute investment in mental clarity? It changed Isabella's life.

By 6:00 AM, I'm hitting the gym. You might wonder what bench presses have to do with mortgages, but let me tell you – this job requires stamina. When I'm going toe-to-toe with underwriters and negotiating better terms for you, I need to be at the top of my game. Every rep, every mile on the treadmill, it's all preparation for going the extra mile for you.

At 7:00 AM, I'm out walking my dogs. This isn't just about getting Fido his exercise – it's my time to ground myself in the real world. As I watch my dogs chase squirrels and greet neighbors, it reminds me that behind every application, every credit score, every debt-to-income ratio, there's a real family with real dreams. It keeps me connected to the human side of what we do.

I remember one morning, as I was walking past a local playground, I saw a mom watching her kids play. It reminded me of Isabella and her dream of a backyard for her kids. That image stayed with me all day, fueling me to push even harder to make her dream a reality.

By 7:30 AM, I'm back home and settling in with my journal. This isn't dear diary stuff – it's where I map out the day's battle plan. I set my intentions, visualize successful outcomes for my clients, and mentally prepare for any challenges that might come up.

On this particular day, I wrote: "Today, I will find a way to make homeownership a reality for Isabella." Setting that intention first thing in the morning kept me focused and determined throughout the day.

At 8:00 AM, I create what I call my Power List. This isn't your average to-do list – it's a strategic plan of attack. I identify the top priorities that will move the needle for my clients. On this day, the top of my list read: "Research alternative loan programs for gig workers – Isabella's file."

From 8:30 AM to 1:00 PM, I'm in what I call my proactive zone. This is where the real magic happens. I'm not just reacting to emails or putting out fires – I'm actively creating opportunities for my clients.

During this time, I dove deep into research about loan programs for gig workers. I called up investors, picked the brains of my network, and even reached out to a fintech startup that was developing new ways to assess creditworthiness for non-traditional workers.

By the end of this proactive time, I had not one but three potential options for Isabella. I felt like a detective who had just cracked a case wide open.

At 1:00 PM, I switch gears. Now, I'm like an ER doctor, ready to diagnose and treat any financial emergencies that come my way. This is when I open myself up to calls, emails, and meetings.

It was during this time that I had my call with Isabella. I could hear the mix of hope and anxiety in her voice as I explained the options I'd found. As I broke down each program, translating the financial jargon into plain English, I could almost hear the weightlifting off her shoulders.

"Reggie," she said, her voice cracking a little, "I can't believe you did all this for me. I thought I was just another application in the pile."

That right there? That's why I do what I do. That's why I wake up at 5:00 AM, why I structure my day the way I do. Because you're never just another application to me. You're a person with dreams, and my entire day is structured around making those dreams a reality.

As the day winds down, I don't just switch off and call it quits. Instead, I take time to reflect on the day's events. I ask myself: Did I add value to my clients' lives today? Were there any challenges that could have been handled more efficiently? What did I learn today that can benefit my clients tomorrow?

On this particular day, I made a note to follow up with that fintech start-up. Their innovative approach to assessing gig worker income could be a game-changer not just for Isabella but for many of my clients.

Finally, as I get ready for bed, I follow a simple routine: I silence my devices, list tomorrow's top priorities, envision successful outcomes for my clients, express gratitude for the day's accomplishments, and prepare my environment for a good night's sleep, pray and go to sleep.

That night, as I laid my head on the pillow, I imagined Isabella and her kids playing in their very own backyard. It brought a smile to my face and renewed my determination to make that vision a reality.

Now, you might be wondering, "Reggie, this all sounds great, but how does your personal routine actually benefit me?" Great question! Let me break it down for you:

1. When you call me, you're getting my full, undivided attention. I'm not juggling a million tasks or trying to multitask – I'm 100% present for you.

2. The time I spend on research and strategy means I'm often solving problems before they even arise in your mortgage journey.

3. Because I take care of my physical and mental health, I have the stamina to go to bat for you, negotiating tirelessly with investors and thinking creatively to overcome obstacles.

4. My evening reflection ensures that the service you receive is constantly evolving and improving.

Every aspect of my day is designed with one goal in mind: to be the best possible advocate for you and your homeownership dreams.

So, as we wrap up this chapter, I want you to remember that success in the mortgage process – and in life – often comes down to the compound effect of small, consistent actions. My daily routine might seem simple, but it's these daily habits, repeated over time, that allow me to provide you with exceptional service.

By sharing my routine with you, I'm not just giving you a peek behind the curtain – I'm inviting you to adopt a mindset of intentionality and continuous improvement in your own life. Whether you're saving for a down payment, improving your credit score, or navigating the complexities of the mortgage application, remember that small, consistent steps can lead to remarkable results.

Are you ready to create your own success routine? Are you prepared to approach your homebuying journey with the same level of intentionality and dedication? If so, then let's synchronize our efforts. With your commitment and my structured approach, we'll create a symphony of success that culminates in the sweet music of you receiving the keys to your new home.

Remember, in the world of mortgages and homeownership, it's not just about working hard – it's about working smart. And with the right daily habits, you can turn your homeownership dreams into reality, one well-structured day at a time. Let's make every day count on your journey to homeownership!

Chapter Seven

Faith, Finance, and Finding Your Path

The 100-Foot Journey

Hey there, future homeowner! We've come a long way together, haven't we? I'm Reggie Williams, and as we wrap up this journey, I want to share something deeply personal with you. It's the spiritual foundation that underlies everything we've talked about so far. As you see, this isn't just about mortgages or homeownership – it's about finding your path in life and understanding how your financial journey fits into the bigger picture.

Let me tell you about Isabella. Isabella came to me a few years back, feeling lost and overwhelmed. She was a single mom with two kids, working two jobs and dreaming of giving her children a stable home. But every time she looked at her bank account or her credit score, that dream seemed to slip further away.

I remember the day she walked into my office. Her shoulders were slumped, her eyes downcast. She looked like she was carrying the weight of the world on her shoulders. "Reggie," she said, her voice barely above a whisper, "I don't know if I can do this. Maybe homeownership just isn't for people like me."

Those words broke my heart, but they also lit a fire in me. Because I knew something Isabella didn't yet understand – that her journey to homeownership was about so much more than just finances; it was about faith, perseverance, and discovering her own inner strength.

So I asked Isabella to sit down, and I shared with her a metaphor that guided me through many dark times. "Imagine," I said, "that you're driving on a dark, winding road. Your headlights only illuminate about 100 feet ahead of you. But you know what? With just that limited visibility, you can successfully drive from Florida to California."

Isabella looked at me, confusion clear on her face. "But Reggie," she said, "what does that have to do with buying a home?"

I smiled. "Everything," I replied. "You see, in life, just like on that dark road, we don't need to see the entire journey to start moving forward. We just need to focus on the next 100 feet."

I could see a glimmer of understanding in Isabella's eyes. So, I pressed on. "Right now, your 100 feet might be improving your credit score. Or maybe it's saving for a down payment. Whatever it is, that's where we need to shine our full attention. Trust me, as you move forward, the path ahead will continue to reveal itself."

Over the next few months, Isabella and I worked together to map out her 100-foot journey. We tackled her credit score, created a savings plan, and started exploring first-time homebuyer programs. But more than that, we worked on building her faith – not just in the process, but in the journey God is taking her on will help reach her destination.

There were times when Isabella felt discouraged. I remember one day when she called me, her voice shaking. She'd just been turned down for a promotion at work, and she felt like it was a sign that she should give up on her dream of homeownership.

That's when I shared with her what I call the 1% rule. "Isabella," I said, "we only have direct control over about 1% of what happens to us. The other

99%? That's in the hands of God, or if you prefer, the complex interplay of countless factors beyond our influence."

"But Reggie," she protested, "doesn't that mean we're powerless?"

"Not at all," I replied. "It means we can stop exhausting ourselves trying to control everything and instead focus our energy on that crucial 1% – our own actions and reactions. You can't control whether you get that promotion, but you can control how you respond to this setback. Will you let it defeat you, or will you use it as motivation to push harder towards your goals?"

I could almost hear the wheels turning in Isabella's mind. And from that day forward, I saw a change in her. She stopped worrying so much about the things she couldn't control and started pouring her energy into the things she could. She picked up extra shifts at work, started a side hustle doing freelance graphic design, and even found creative ways to cut her expenses.

But Isabella's journey wasn't just about financial growth. As we worked together, I saw her spiritual growth as well. She started practicing gratitude, finding joy in the small victories along the way. Each time her credit score went up a few points or she hit a savings milestone, we celebrated. These weren't just financial wins – they were stepping stones in her personal growth.

I remember the day Isabella called me, excitement bubbling in her voice. "Reggie," she said, "I just realized something amazing. This journey... it's changing me. I'm not just working towards a house. I'm becoming a stronger, more confident person."

That's when I shared with her the concept of sanctification – the idea that life is a continual process of growth and refinement. "Every challenge you face," I told her, "Is an opportunity for growth. Every setback is a chance to learn resilience. Every success is a stepping stone to even greater achievements."

As Isabella's journey continued, I saw her start to pay it forward. She began sharing what she was learning with her coworkers, encouraging them to take control of their finances. She volunteered at a local financial literacy program, helping others who were where she had been just a few months before.

"You know, Reggie," she told me one day, "I used to think that I needed to achieve my goals before I could help others. But now I realize that helping others is helping me achieve my goals. It's like... the more I give, the more I receive."

I couldn't have been prouder. Isabella was discovering one of life's most beautiful truths – that our journey isn't just about us. As we navigate our path, we have the opportunity to create positive ripples that extend far beyond our own lives.

Finally, after months of hard work, ups and downs, tears and triumphs, we reached the day of Isabella's closing. As we sat at that table, surrounded by stacks of papers, I watched Isabella's hand as she signed her name. Her fingers weren't shaking anymore. There was a strength and confidence in her movements that hadn't been there when we first met.

After the final document was signed, Isabella looked up at me, her eyes shining with tears of joy. "Reggie," she said, "I did it! I did it! I own a home."

I smiled back at her, feeling my own eyes get a little misty. "No, Isabella," I replied. "You did so much more than that. You transformed your life. This home? It's just the beginning."

As we walked out of the closing, I asked Isabella to reflect on her journey. "If you could go back and tell yourself one thing when we first met," I said, "what would it be?"

Isabella thought for a moment, then smiled. "I'd tell myself that happiness is a choice," she said. "No matter how tough things get, I have the power to choose joy, to choose gratitude, and to keep moving forward."

I couldn't have said it better myself. Because that, my friend, is one of life's most profound truths. Regardless of your circumstances, you have the power to choose your emotional state. This doesn't mean ignoring life's challenges or pretending everything is perfect. Instead, it's about finding joy and gratitude even amidst difficulties.

Now, as we conclude our time together, I want you to think of this book not as an endpoint but as the beginning of your own 100-foot journey. You don't need to see the entire path to homeownership and financial wellness. You just need to take the next step.

Maybe your next step is reaching out to start the pre-approval process. Perhaps it's creating a budget to boost your savings. Or it could be as simple as spending some quiet time reflecting on what homeownership truly means to you.

Whatever that next step is, I encourage you to take it with faith, focus, and a choice to be happy. Remember, you're not just buying a house – you're creating a home, building wealth, and writing a new chapter in your life story.

As you move forward, keep in mind the lessons from Isabella's journey:

1. Focus on the next 100 feet. You don't need to see the entire road to start moving forward.

2. Remember the 1% rule. Focus your energy on what you can control – your own actions and reactions.

3. Embrace the process of growth. Every challenge is an opportunity to become stronger.

4. Pay it forward. Your journey can inspire and help others.

5. Choose happiness. No matter what circumstances you face, you have the power to choose your emotional state.

As we part ways (at least in the pages of this book), I want you to know that your journey doesn't end here. Whether you're ready to start the homebuying process now or someday in the future, know that I'm here as your lifelong ally.

My commitment to you goes beyond just securing a mortgage. I'm here to support your entire financial journey, to celebrate your successes, to help you navigate challenges, and to cheer you on every step of the way.

Remember, in the grand tapestry of life, your home is more than just a financial investment – it's a sanctuary for your dreams, a launchpad for your aspirations, and a legacy for future generations. And I consider it my life's purpose to help you achieve that.

So, are you ready to take the next step on your 100-foot journey? Are you prepared to move forward with faith, focus, and a positive mindset? If so, then let's embark on this adventure together. With trust in the journey and a commitment to growth, there's no limit to what you can achieve.

Thank you for allowing me to be part of your journey. Here's to your bright future, your beautiful home, and the incredible life you're building – one faith-filled step at a time. Let's make your dreams of making money while you sleep a reality & building a lifelong family legacy a reality!